Smoked Pearl

Poems of Hong Kong and Beyond

Akin Jeje

Inaugural Proverse Prize Semi-Finalist

Smoked Pearl is Akinsola Olufemi Jeje's first full-length collection of poetry, a semi-autobiographical compilation of poems written between 2005 and 2008. The collection thus indirectly chronicles Jeje's arrival in Hong Kong and his subsequent observations of Hong Kong life, Chinese and world events (Canada, Iraq, Africa, the USA); and his musings on race, culture, everyday life and matters of the heart. By turns exuberant, pensive, angry and poignant, *Smoked Pearl* speaks from the heart of a black Westerner as he negotiates the complexities of "Asia's world city" and its unique place in Chinese history and culture. Akin Jeje sees Hong Kong as a place where the political intersects with the personal. In his poetry, he compellingly shows his consciousness that the territory itself creates its own daily poetry through the joined rhythms of its own existence and that of the emerging giant on whose lip it rests. The title "Smoked Pearl" alludes to Hong Kong's position at the mouth of China's Pearl River Delta. But it also calls to mind Hong Kong's common designation as, "the Pearl of the Orient", indicating that here we have a different view. Jeje brings to Hong Kong and the world events he engages with a unique perspective of outrage, fascination, and – ultimately – compassion.

Supported by

香港藝術發展局
Hong Kong Arts Development Council

The Hong Kong Arts Development Council fully supports freedom of artistic expression. The views and opinions expressed in this project do not represent the stand of the Council.

Smoked Pearl

Poems of Hong Kong and Beyond

Akin Jeje

Proverse Hong Kong

Smoked Pearl: Poems of Hong Kong and Beyond
by Akin Jeje.
2nd pbk edition published in Hong Kong by Proverse Hong Kong,
December 2015.
Copyright © Proverse Hong Kong, December 2015.
ISBN: 978-988-8228-20-1
Printed by CreateSpace

1st published in pbk in Hong Kong by Proverse Hong Kong, November 2010.
Copyright © Proverse Hong Kong, 23 November 2010.
ISBN: 978-988-19321-1-2

1st edition Distribution (Hong Kong and worldwide):
Chinese University Press of Hong Kong, Chinese University of Hong Kong,
Shatin, NT, Hong Kong SAR.
Tel: [INT+852] 3943-9800; Fax: [INT+852] 2603-7355
E-mail: cup-bus@cuhk.edu.hk Web: www.chineseupress.com

Enquiries: Proverse Hong Kong, P.O. Box 259, Tung Chung Post Office,
Tung Chung, Lantau, NT, Hong Kong SAR.
Web: www.proversepublishing.com

The right of Akin Jeje to be identified as the author of
Smoked Pearl: Poems of Hong Kong and Beyond has been asserted by him
in accordance with the Copyright, Designs and Patents Act 1988.

Cover image, courtesy Martyn Gregory Gallery.
Cover design by Proverse Hong Kong and Artist Hong Kong Company.
Page design, copy-editing and proof-reading by Proverse Hong Kong.

British Library Cataloguing in Publication Data.
A catalogue record for the 1st edition of this title
is available from the British Library

Note on the cover image
Chinese artist, c. 1800 (courtesy Martyn Gregory Gallery)

The following careful explanation, describing the mixture of Chinese and western techniques that the artist portrayed in the cover image is using, as well as the fact that the Chinese artist, at an early stage of the meeting of east and west, is copying a portrait of a western woman for the overseas market (i.e. beyond Asia), sets up a fascinating conversation with *Smoked Pearl: Poems of Hong Kong and Beyond*, where a black westerner paints with words his early and developing responses to the people and proceedings of Hong Kong.

"The Chinese artist is working on a reverse-glass painting for the Western market. His right wrist rests on a flat strip of wood placed across the frame, to prevent the artist from cracking the glass; his oil paints are arranged western-style on an oval palette, but he holds his brush in the traditional Chinese style. The British artist William Alexander, visiting a Cantonese 'export' artist's studio in December 1793, noted that 'Painting on the back of Glass is much in vogue here, on this substance where the picture requires it, they reverse the subject dexterously enough'. ... The artist seems to be copying a portrait of a Western woman."

(Catalogue No. 86, "The Art of the China Trade", Martyn Gregory Gallery, 2010-11, p. 81.)

Truths Murmured in Twilight: the Many Voices of Akin Jeje

Akin Jeje's début collection is shaded in the tones of evening: from the polluted glow of Hong Kong's skies; through "mist-swooned black" and "burnt haze" to "embers over coals". Fires that flash hidden depths are seen in muted evenings, in tarnished silver light. The observations here are cool, wry, sometimes detached, but always reverent. Those fortunate to have seen Jeje perform in Hong Kong, in any of his voices, in any of his twilights, will recognise the silhouettes formed by the "crowd through the smoke-lit richness//of the endless evening". We know that his writing frames a multiplicity of voices and registers: just as there is room in his heart both for the polluted skies of Hong Kong and the "big sky vast earth breadth burst melt" of his native Canada. He writes, as so many of us must, of writing itself: his "reprisin' life in voluminous webs" in the poem 'words on a page' – and here, too, is the glow: the pages of his poetry gleaming through denim under the ultra-violet of nightclubs and hotspots.

For Jeje sees the gleam revealed within the grime: his titular smoked pearl evocative of this interplay of light and dark. For tarnished things must once have been precious, and though Jeje writes of wasted days, he recognises the briefness, "the glory of the blaze."

This book in so many ways is an act of worship, whether it be the ever-diminishing words of love and fear framed in the pointed brevity of text message, or an elegiac reminder of humankind's capability for tragedy, wherever we are and wherever we call home. Jeje's work draws us back to the darkness: college shootings, war crimes in Rwanda and all that "should never have been". In the Tiananmen-inspired 'may days for june the fourth', the poet reminds us of our shared culpability and loss: "ask not for whom the blood flows", the poem riffs: "it flows for we."

The "we" here is signal, for the underlying message of *Smoked Pearl* is inclusion, and shared responsibility. Jeje, like many English-language writers in Hong Kong, is an expatriate, an outsider looking in, and yet the poet, like the reader, is never merely an observer. In much of Jeje's work, the personal becomes the political: his meditations on the "ancient rites" of Southeast Asian (Filipino, Indonesian and Thai) prostitutes culminate in the re-figuring of the ultimate Oriental pleasure-girl in 'Suzie Redux', a rueful but reverent reflection on the nature of sexual politics in so much of Asia. Jeje gives voice to those who do not speak up, whether they be the "teak-hued" domestic helpers of Hong Kong, or the nameless victims of shopping mall shootings in his native Canada.

But for all that Jeje sees – the injustice, the silence and the blame – these darknesses of the human soul are not total: the night ends, hope dawns. The defining mood of the collection can be located in the delicately etched portrait 'Mother and child', "I finally saw something good tonight." And this blooming of optimism is also reflected in the shifts of the world stage: the poet looks to the presidency of Barack Obama as the beginnings of light, seen, as always, through the filter of Hong Kong's "inevitable wash//of faded figures" – bootleg T-shirts of famous faces.

As twilight marks the boundary between day and night, so Jeje's work shifts as his writing blurs between poetry and prose. Smoked Pearl ends with the poem "here..." with the tangible presence of the new day, new love and all the hope promised therein:

"We are
here."

Viki Holmes
Hong Kong, October 2010

Author of *miss moon's class*
and co-editor, with Kate Rogers,
of the international women's poetry anthology *Not A Muse*.

CB

CR

Table of Contents

Smoked Pearl

൙

Author's Acknowledgments

When I first started this book, I was encouraged in this project by a number of people and organizations whom I would like to thank.

Outloud Poetry and the Joyce's Collective in Hong Kong helped me with my motivation to write. Rob and Joyce Baker provided and still provide space and time at Joyce's Bar and Café, "Joyce is not Here", so that poets can have a space to express themselves. The monthly poetry event, OutLoud, held at the Hong Kong Festival Fringe, is invaluable for providing the opportunity to reach an audience and the sense of a community of poets: I thank particularly some of its organizers – Madeleine Slavick, David McKirdy, Martin Alexander, Jason Lee – as well as the fellow poets whom I meet there. Among them, Kate Rogers, both fellow poet and fellow Canadian and also fellow poet Viki Holmes (also of Jazzetry), have each provided me with advice, support and friendship. I am especially grateful to Viki for writing the Preface to this book. Novelist Xu Xi provided advice and support, pushing me to improve my craft. I thank Xu Xi and also author, Yeeshan Yang, for writing encouraging words about my book.

I want to thank fellow members of the Joyce's Collective: Andy Barker, Jason Lee, Tom Grundy, Rosie McLoughlin, Selina Lai, Aaliya Zaveri, Paul Ulrich, Blair Reeve, David Hill, Benjamin Mackie, Keith Mullen, Nashua Gallagher and Angus Gallagher, Mary-Jane Newton and many others for being my irrepressible poet brothers and sisters, inspiring others with their verse.

I would like to express my gratitude to my editor and publisher Gillian Bickley, who has guided me through this project from its inception, and also to Verner Bickley and Proverse Hong Kong, my publishers.

I say thank you to Nashua Gallagher, a valiant poet and good friend who helped me edit this book, along with another good friend Reid Mitchell: their combined efforts helped my manuscript achieve the long list for the 2009 Proverse Prize.

I am most grateful for a grant in support of publication from the Hong Kong Arts Development Council.

Most of all, I want to thank my father, Ayodeji Jeje, for encouraging me to read and explore, to see the world as I see it now; my mother, Saeeda Jeje, whom I write about in the first poem in this book; and my beautiful wife Arsenia Amoranto Jeje, who – though she doesn't care for poetry – cares for me, and has been a pillar of support. In addition, I thank my stepson Justin for being his wonderful self, and the Amoranto/Feniza family for being my second family. Last but not least, I would like to thank my younger brother Yemisi Jeje, who continues to be a source of strength, compassion, and goodness for me in my struggles to understand the complexities of life itself.

Author's Introduction

Smoked Pearl is a compilation of poems I wrote between September 2005, when I first arrived in Hong Kong, and January 2009, during the inauguration of America's first black president. *Smoked Pearl*, although ostensibly about my observations and experiences in Hong Kong, transcends this view, for in this world of internet access, 24-hour news and instant information, the scope of the poems goes further, towards mainland China, Asia, Africa, Canada, the Western world, and ultimately, to an elusive place called home. The poems deal with a variety of subject matter, from culture shock and political upheaval, through the social ills of prostitution and poverty in an emerging Asia, to the most personal of matters, a single man's experiences with love, cultural adjustment and emotional alienation.

Despite the wide range of my subject matter, I do not purport to have definitive answers for what I have seen, felt, and write about: – I, after all, am one person, with a singular point of view, informed by my identity as a foreigner in Hong Kong, a Canadian far away from home, and a black man trying to make sense of a Western-and-Asian dominated world. My literary influences were men and women like Senegal's Leopold Senghor, Martinique's Aimé Césaire, Nigeria's Wole Soyinka and America's Langston Hughes and Rita Dove, all of whose works straddle the intersection between the personal and the political, and do so in verse rich with imagery, pain and compassion.

I can only hope to follow their illustrious footsteps, but I am encouraged by something a friend once told me concerning poetry and readers' reaction towards it: "It may be sharp, it may be tawdry, it may be angry, it even may be over-effusive; but it is poetry if it makes readers react, whether with pleasure or anger, inspiration or disgust. The worst poetry is poetry that leaves readers indifferent".

Smoked Pearl

I will say only this – I would like to have readers of this book enjoy my verse, hope to arouse their ire with some of the things I write about, pray that I will inspire someone out there to speak out or do something that will better our world, and know that I will disgust some who have radically different viewpoints from mine. The only fear I have is to leave the readers indifferent.

**For my Grandfather
Chief Michael Akinsola Jeje
(1919-2006)**

CB

Mama

The horned glasses –
tortoise-shell, bright and gleaming,
were all that remained
constant;
a shuffle rather than stride;
smooth cheeks caressed
into distant lands'
unknown planes, deep an' wizened;
warm silica grin conceals
the barbs in back; the
varicose veins
brightly garbed
in *uhuru* caftan.

Of course, much has changed
for the one whose
baked cashew hue
resembles mine.

When I was a child, just before dark, she would
read baby Yemi and me
ancient tales of the mighty sun, the endless
earth, the brilliance of the sky.

Now it is I
who sends these tales
in electronic blips
to an old woman

Smoked Pearl

separated from iⁱ
by
the setting sun
an endless ocean
and the vastness
of the sky.

Aviary Pagoda

At night
'specially
Mist-swooned black
On the tower block

A queenly pagoda, feathered in battle green sheaves
And concrete girders,
Reminds of dreams

In solitude, aloof from the crumbling project blocks

Nestled in brushes and brambles and thickets of chirps,
coos

On a deep emerald hill

Amongst all the bangcantowailclatter

That clutters
The neon-strewn cracked roads

A moment's blind, soft quietude, before a descent
To purgatory.

For Caleb Jordan[ii]

Strange irony
Indeed

When the beloved young
Pass
Suddenly

Leaving old and corrupt like i
To linger

The first awareness, in the house of the Lord
My first day there
Was of
His death

Pain crackling torn emotional
Through hushed pews
Weeping women
Worn faced pastor, eyes welled red storm
Mouth grim

But, brothers it was not all bitter,
This feeling that cascaded the crowded hall

All that loved him,
From every one of God's nations,
Began to re-weave
Broken strands
Tales warmed
By light and love

Smoked Pearl

Of the beauty
Strength
Essential goodness
Of the man
Taken too soon
Never forgotten

I saw, for next week's bulletin

A last picture
Eyes deep and kind
Carriage tall and lean
Visage lit
With the blessing of a divine power
Compassionate, serene
At rest, wearing
An endearing 'aw shucks' grin

Hustler's Prayer

blessed be the almighty game
even if it has brought nought
but pain, slivers and shivers tremblin' in the shame

bright gold early mornin'
glad an' hibiscus sweet
momentarily
peels crimson-heavy eyes
singed ivory grins

that return grim
thoughts veering
into dark-hue deeps

after-love already spilt
and mourn
for what was
just to survive

but we will, my beloveds,

to thrive,
in the gritty city
of the almighty game.

Shenzhou VI[iii]

First Asians in space, the PRC
the final frontier, once Taiwan returns
into its
appropriate slot.

Higher, faster, stronger –
the credo
of any emerging empire,

vast empty expanses, a
challenge too untamed
to resist.

For every challenge
a challenger, a discovery,
one the politburo felt
this once
would escape dissension

or perhaps not.

Tibetan herdsman, Xinjiang nomad, Shanghai socialite,
Beijing office clerk alike,

Watching the reachable skies;

One, wondering at the cost,
looks forlornly at the rags on his back,
and the leanness of his scruffy sheep.

One, questioning if questions, thoughts, ideas
would ever be allowed,
to be as galaxial as the conquest of space.

Smoked Pearl

One, in trepidation at the thought
of electronic eyes,
in the skies
vigilant, unblinking, unmerciful.

And one, who wishes
The Party's pride
would come burning down,
Violently,
in a meteoric shower
of sizzling débris.

Tremors

Faces, least to mine; eyes
Flat, simian, unsmiling, surly

That, with the harsh sing-song
Impresses first-timers naught

With the *inscrutable* put-on, that masks

The mutual incense burning;

Fear, distrust, barely veiled hostility
Steaming
Through
The cracks

Torn by cultural tremors.

Smoked Pearl

It's slightly warm, this swirling
smoked pearl
with its fragrant cacophony
sci-fi rushing limbs, irate horns, frying wok oil,
high-pitched screams and opulence,
Benz stars and LV straps in chaotic profusion
gorgeous from a distance—usually of the postcard kind—
but a delicate, and peculiarly sensitive bauble to handle…

a humid patina of tropical dampness competes with the
burnt haze, staining the lustre of its face,

—continuously tumultuous—
as the fragrant pearl's sheen,

and I wonder how the hell, if at all

I add to its glow.

French Riots '05

even from
far Pacific reaches

one can feel burning, sirens, roars
in QuickTime ™

soon enough,
a moltenrubber acrid cloud
of braggadocious bile

will come to a place near you,
hissing putridly with every hue
of a leaden rainbow.

Fortresses that define borders with a furtive clutch, a
passing sneer
and *banlieues* far from the centre
should expect such reactions, as *Le establishment* totters
one step from decline, as the *blackblancbeurs* crowd the
opposite line.

What happens to a dream
that never was?

Does it stain social fabric
A hue of old Bordeaux?

Or guillotines in the mist
Awaiting convulsions in *le métro*?

'Cause they're now screamin'
To fucking hell with the heavy load
This *salope* is gon'explode!

Ping Shan Heritage Trail

Only an act of pragmatism
keeps this journey
of pre-Hong Kong
alive.

Ten frayed monuments
in solemn succession,
like those
parchment-faced grandmas
tottering gradually through
e-impatient crowds.

Little feeling
from the bustle; ignoring what's past
few here
treasure relics without a price.
Temples graying, village walls thick with moss,
dusted curios,
rusted paths,
final memoriam of a forgotten age.

Kids pass noisily
eyes intent on hand-held Game Boys™
I the foreign, the only face
searching in vain, through newness
for secrets in stone skulls and gaudy sages,
somewhere in the emerald rust of copper shingles.

The last stop.
Back to the station, to life.
Leave the Ping Shan Trail as an after-forethought.

Smoked Pearl

Nestled in hills
even I won't recall myself,
given time, and the
usual uncaring.

About a Girl

O dear Lord,
That ol' time feelin'
that I never'd thought
would reach in ever again.
Thousands of miles runnin' in exile,
Up 22 more stories in the shelterin' sky,
in I,

Starts to creep,
Infiltrate an inner empire,
like a divine wind.

Please no black storm number 8, no rise
to swellcrash, fury sweet
sweeping, scouring,

The last of I
that didn't remain behind,

Out in a China South sea
South China sea
sea South China,

reflecting the twisting currents
of her oceanic eyes.

Everything but the Girl

Sorry no can do. Thanks anyways.

was as conclusive

in electronic script

as a final sentence.

Firm. Dismissive. Ultimate. Uninterested.

Staring

At the tiny screen

No comfort
Reading
Absence

In the lit expanse

That refuses

To say

Any more.

After Hotel Rwanda

This is what I thought

Last credits

Mambazo township voices lifted

loud and keen, a dirge blended with relief

Nigger,

I was born to die in pain

But my grave is bare
Even in name.

Millions
Whose bones flower in liana rot, mud-heavy fields
fertilizing sharpened petals for future conflict

On a continent the pristine world ignores

as irredeemable,
except

For a handful of suited saints,
the rest of the cast set in bone-thin pathos,
or grimaces beneath war-paint…

Blessed Come...

Blessed come the new year,

with burning pitch
scorching lungs
and veins

poisons of five thousand eves
past,[iv]
hone the razor bite of
withdrawal pains.

Etching elaborate tattoos of lustillusion,
despairconfusion,

with a future promise, a power
of the unconquerable, the undefeatable

adorned such
sometimes crawling
sometimes leaping

towards the sign
of a luminous cross...

Smoked Pearl

At nights,

Heaves and moans,
raven-haired, bronze-burnish
platinum, cream-gloss
auburn, russet-glaze,
jet-spill, daffodil
burnt curls, onyx sheen,
lacquered up,

still open,
to bare the maw
bare the all
drawing nearer…

Eaton Centre Shootings (Toronto, Canada)[v]
Boxing Day, 26 December 2005.

They say
that some gunfaya,
spittin' fury like a rudebwai
'pan a mike
can be heard
round the globe.

Well, 9mm shells
sprayed 'round
the Eaton Centre,
bustin' vessels
and Christmas cheer alike,
piercing the armour
of my distant world, in foreign.

It's on, now.
Young niggas lickin' shots hit
The worst victim possible;
She was fifteen,
Well-to-do, by the clothes strewn
from the bags,
And blonde.
Naturally.
With the eyes and face to match.

First sign.
Of Rebirthin' a Nation.

T.O.'s mood is sombre, brooding;
Calls for law and order garbled with cries for peace, for
understanding,
An ominous clarion for action,
I'm sure long overdue.

Smoked Pearl

But it'll come down
on yardies first, yes, but ultimately
Any nigger's head;
More niggers resistin' arrest,
more shot tryin' to escape,
Naturally, more dead.

These ones here dem catch will be filling out, no parole;
A life's bid,
For once again, losing they heads.

A hard blue sweep back
Into the darkened corners,
Of the mosaic city.
Later –

Killings will continue,
'pan the dancehall.
Terrified dark forms
will remain shadows
to the riddim and staccato
of the rattle of gunfaya

Resuming
Self-hate
Unchecked, unheeded,
their type, troublesome as a group, and therefore unneeded.

And mine eyes,
Weary of the strain,
Shift back, from the on-lined
Reports,
back to the corner of my book.

Pattaya

A magnificent concentration
(just like a camp)

of all that is…well…
Tawdry, sleazy, counterfeit, hot, noisome, indolent,
bothersome but somehow so demimonde alluring, a last
thrust, a sudden sweet spurt, and cooling of the soggy after-
mess.

Indeed a furtive mating,
Low-scale BangkokPatpong, SoutheastAsianRio,
Glitter like Vegas hustle all Macau-bluster, like a pre-
Katrina N'Orleans, supple teak skins and spilt Singha brew
swells the womb of the nation, for better or worse…

Less charitable accounts
compare this cut-rate nirvana
and its sixty thousand souls,
after the tourist hordes,
to the scatterings of a stench-filled bowl.

After all, everyone – from black Khmer, cocoa Laos and
cinnamon Thais
to quivering pale Russians, phlegmatic Brits, and ruddy
Germans – arrive
to expel their waste,
with their stress, their frustrations,
their poisons on the damned here.

Out here, don't cost
too much more
than the 5 baht, to expel
what ails.

Smoked Pearl

Long as someone's collecting,
Long lines at the terminal,

Silvercoins and bundlenotes,

Still much heavier
so far
than the mass of stench

Left behind
Damned, short skirts, black killer eyes, and broad, brown
smiles,
still enticing in the humid velvet of the Gulf night.

Tik

Conscience is part of the process

We spent four out of the eight nights together

One alone, two with another, a dive and thrust with a third

But it was more

than a joining of rented flesh.

Eyes darker than the humid Thai night
Shielding the horrors of her life

Loving all her sisters of the night
at the sign of the Silk Ribbon,

Thai princess of the gutter
Never would I utter
a syllable against her

Would have been my girl
if I actually lived here,
in this chipped, glittery edge
of the Gulf of Siam

Tresses, spilled oil
Cheekbones, Nefertiti
Hue milk tea,
Hiked dresses, razor stiletto heels

Smoked Pearl

Ridin' and dyin'
with the rest of her girls,
Female bodies adorned
with the tapestry of their suffering;
Tattoos, blotches, bruises, stretch marks
from the infants of illicit love.

Was I a monster,
for being with her a few days?

Midnight love lingers in my thoughts

Drawn, torn by the dilemma.

Survivor

This is for an old lady in the park, practising her morning
tai chi exercises.

Bespectacled, as they used to say,
Rotund, matronly.

Energetic hand blows,
Arm flows,
Sweeping the morning mist,

On the deserted soccer court
Crowned with steel fences,

Age spots, sports pants,
A shiny patterned silk
Barrel chest,
Short, gleaming black crown
Vaguely Maoesque.

Stretches and yawns
serenely into the
sky-dawning morning.
Amidst the growing bustle,
Peace in the maelstrom.

Watching her carry out her
Daily exercise routine,
I marveled at her tranquility

And wondered
At the ordeals
she may have seen.

Lent in Hong Kong

One night, a boy, hair a-halo, strums a guitar outside the
methadone clinic with his friends. The day is the start of
Lent.

The best thing, THE best thing
we ever done,
Was squat, squat outside the
methadone clinic,
With the sufferheads
Worn and withdrawn,

To sing songs of freedom.

One had eyes closed,

Hands clasped in
Shuddering visual ecstasy, perhaps
For lives lost in his private haze.

Villagers, walking past
Shaking, clucking, clutching hurriedly money to be
preserved only for the deserving

As we, small, devout knot of *gweilos*

Seated on smeared concrete,

continued singing songs of freedom.

Easter on the Pearl

Finally,
Gently toasting off layers of

The grim-grey industrial haze

Are the first sun-drenched fumes
Of moistened warmth,
Ripe Bauhinia, startling blood crimson
Electric exciting
On cracked cement blocks,
Riven by haste and error,
Welcoming the richness of the scent.

A more embracing season arrives
Without firecracker scarlet-gold,
or thick-wad-notes prosperity

Glass-cathedrals, monuments of cement,
Steel monsters coated
A metallic mandarin melting
Into the rust,
Stacks of white-washed iron bins
are new temples of commerce out here,
charged with idols'
fiscal intensity,
That shall never erase the sun (son)
sun (son)
sun (son)

And the many gifts
Of re-awakening.

Earth Day in HK

Earth day in HK
could be considered irony
In a land of rubble, old and new
Steel pillars held aloft by splintering bamboo spikes,
themselves bolstered by the whiff
of open, sulphurous drains,

that paradoxically, nourish the last wide-leafed
banana trees of the villages, which like green patches about
to be furrowed, will be

stripped to a scabrous purple;
Rivers bricked, ghostyards corrugated,
Roofs rotted to the dampness of sodden thatch;

iron and stone and plastic and bones,
Littering the last scrubs
Of forest and field

In the name of economic survival.

The land still breathes, in wheezes and gasps,
with seven million on its chest,
But over the Lo Wu, well over a billion

wait to be finally seated at the table of prosperity.

The earth itself may live to see another rebirth;
but soon, in HK, this day may be set aside,
less celebration than opprobrium,

with momentum towards memoriam.

Suzie Redux

I know the world
Of Suzie Wong
But that's not what
They call her any more
She prefers these days
A one-word
Love handle.

OR, TIK, MERLIE, FELICIA, ANGEL
Any of the others
That grace browner seas,
To the south…

There are other terms –
WhorebitchsluthookercuntpussyasssnatchgashLBFMskins
–

A slap, a raw angry burst
And it's out the door,
Hustling, slavering for that one…two…five thousand,
Sweet cream, depending on the night
Girth of waist, broadness of wallet;

Sisterhood of mercy,
Only protection
From the hoods, the sharp-eyed Cantonese madams,
Greedy uniforms,
Three eyed metallic razor norms; hustle, pay up, and
conform.

Smoked Pearl

One night,
We drank off the clock
Enough, to begin to see the trickles,
Real name, hometown,
Family chatter, birthday;
Other tiny sweetnesses in the gloom;
Tiger eyes, luminous dark,
Crystallined with spearm
Not yet I-ced,
Admittedly, some of it was practiced,
Survival instincts die real hard.

Hesitations ever so slight, however,
shredded silences between the banter,
grasping fingers, neither trusting
the other, to say what the other
really felt.

Walked her back, harsh-red neon glares
a public kiss bye.
Left, mistrust rippling through the longing

for the girl
behind the glitter stare and
freshly-smeared lipgloss,

striding forth
to repeat

her ancient rites.

A Dream of Canadian Plains

In the dream I saw
Thousands of ice-white droplets,
brilliant-clear quartz shards,
diamond sparkles, glass beads,
spraying fountains astride the expanse of
gnarled brambles and blades of grass frosted an acid lime –

As the plains secured in the valley of my mind, I recalled;

the snow-crust, aged, hardened
somewhat soiled
from the last of the prairie earth
and sprigs of spent pasture, bent and browned
warmed for final dissolution

Big sky, vast earth breadth burst melt, beautiful, cotton-
streaked
startling sapphire horizon.

an ecstasy, the liberation of the
Great bright North alive.

Washing, thawing, greening, the part of home adored

then I re-awake into … exile.

My Girl's a ...

My girl
is a whore
My whore, their whore
Our whore, I guess.
My whore, is well,
I'm not sure.

But the war of petals and thorns
has begun
in earnest, cruelty and tenderness

Leopard stares and caresses complete with honey drippin'
claws.

as a child I was told

to love my enemy,
to forgive my enemy,
to succour my enemy,

The problem, my brothers,
is that I do.

Jenny

ah bredren!

my core bleed
with pity, desire, anger an' churnin' shame
when I enter 'pan the dancehall
with all the gyal dem hustlin'!

She had her fine blond braids tight,
War paint, rosy-eyes set
hard, even 'gainst me.

Struttin' with her girls
just as cold-smile,
just as evil-eye,

Queen of the trashy neon,
fuschia-tight baby doll dress,
brazenly attempt to impress,
the badman dem wid' her malay sashay,

But as she chatter, roll her
globes, pose and mutter,

it remind me
of a pair a' high heels,
a closet, a mother far away,
and a lickle girl
preenin', stumblin'
preenin', stumblin'
in dem glamorous high heels.

Holiday Accident[vi]

roadside
merriment abruptly cut
a headlong smask
twisted metal strips gleaming

in the Thai sun,
smoked glass webbed by
cracks and splinters,
shaken bodies, a few strewn
wails, sirens, sobs
lifted keen sharp piercing
above the milling crowds.

It was meant
as a warm-drenched relief,
from a routine of smog and tar,
lives of papers, stresses, strains,
but such is unpredictability
under God's vast earth.

A moment's slip –
of a large rubber spoke
had two large sedate coaches
under the Thai sun
whimper so in pain.

That Old School Beat

bring, that beat back
bring that, beat back
bring that beat, back
bring that beat back,

'cause I'm tired of burglar alarms
ringin'
an' funeral choirs singin'
platinum-encrusted fools swingin'
mics like maces
destroying lives, burying our faces
in the rancid mud
of their lyrics awash wid murder-money-power-rape

that's why I write this here jason's lyric[vii]
for our dead,
and the lives they misled.

Bring that beat back, that feel back, that groove, that love,
that slow-jam hold-her-need-her, send me whipappeal,
gritty, gunky get down, james brown, black and proud
Motown, what's goin' on move on up, givin' me somethin' I
can feel, sound,

before it all walks on by,

drownin' in the madness.

Dragon Boat at Stanley

Sootsweatsauna

Steams
Over the jagged faces
Of peaks and crowds today

Armies straining over swells
Exhale, chant, exhale, chant
Clang exhale clang chant clangclang
Clang clang...
Spewing scarlet glow golden fire
On the chemical greyness
Of harbours and channels
Pleasure boats watching
Baby's got Chanel
Sippin' import outa funnels
Owned by the company
Not for hire
Sitting atop the economic spire

But alas
Not such a public event, really

Privilege has its membership

News 2006 – a Contrast in Games

I read the news today,
and indeed, it had the hue of smeared, splotched ink so
deeply stained that naught could wash pain from fingers
and eyes that read the
nineteenth explosion this week, the 2,651st soldier to be
sliced to yellow ribbons round the old oak tree, the 100,
000th veiled child to be lifted in bits and parts, high above
the shattering minaret, the muezzin's howl of agony

the next burned through the first,
embers over coals, shone with hope a black star blazing
stampeding legs flying furious over pitch white spiral
hurtling triumph twice hitting squares white nylon laces
yaaaaaay!!!!!! yaaaaaayyyy!!!!
flags waving crowd ecstatic
eagle banners, rainbow banners, stripes and stars in
competition not conflict crosses red snow yellow aqua and
a bright brave galaxy on a topaz diamond in an emerald
forest king of the beautiful game ignites multitudes
disparate to blaze firelight fervour

horrors and wonders
that will unknown
over times
fade to white

Golden Coast

In the beginning was a dream,
sittin' with the girls golden humid coast evening
on the furthest shores of *Heung Gong*
the first time I ever thought they were beautiful,
at peace, finally, the most stressed out sisterhood
I ever seen besides the daughters of Wanchai
Ten months of high pitch nasal ring-clang

Cantonese assaulting my ears
Ten months of misunderstandings, recriminations and fears
Mutual antagonism, I thought, in the ringing silence
between the words
Quietude revealing truths in the velvet lush evening
The first time I thought all, sisterhood of children
Mothers for thousands
That they were, in their almond-eyed endurance
Ever so beautiful

As I Thought of Her

It's a
willie hutch groove
warm molasses keening
I choose you baby, melting in
absence.

A Rest

burning
fetters cracking
walking free breathing free
glorious is the first reprieve
from toil.

Departure

crack'd grins
at the café
whose faces will depart
shortly. A last hurrah, drunk in
Silence.

Shui Pin Wai Estate

this morning, the bright
gold sun rained white fire
on the milling crowds.

mute, hard faces grim,
they board, tread, spit and cackle

strong limbs, wizened backs

in any other
place it would be a
run down ghetto slum

ambition, perhaps,
is what keeps the estate clean,
alive, tenacious

even though, there's times
where I hear sharp cleavers
snap into shocked backs

Papa gone real mad
Ma and kids' howls

Investigation

reveals that he went
mad with stress silver slash
domestic sound clash

a back page story
as crowds teem forth on their way
to various lives.

Me and Michelle

after the night of the living wineheads
three hysterical texts, seven in the mornin'
to a woolly, poundin' skull
screamin' *I never wanna see you again*
this is happenin' too fast
can we be friends I hope you understand
it's okay you didn' do anything wrong
I know you are kind—just as jumbled as the situation
she went incognegro— sixty miles right down to zero. I
went victor to anti-hero.

three weeks later,
numerous unanswered
calls, sped electronic clicks
in her unfathomable dark

finally gamed on
to meet this Nihonjin bijin, this Tokyo fine-lady
that I'll call Reiko (you know, rhymes with Seiko)
lounging with, slinky lights neon at Q's upstairs
sippin' an' smokin' and lightly strokin' arms
after toil, a labour of delicious play
my almond grin, her burnt auburn eyes, our kaleidoscopic
limbs on display

As we was leaving,
a nuclear blast back for all those lost little clicks,
electrons in her atomsphere – my phone rang hard, sudden.
Surprise! – it was her
calling *darlin' sweet baby hi where are you missed you*
spider sense buzzing furiously for the disturbance in the
force
that a next *biatch* must be causin' for her galaxy, unseen

Smoked Pearl

so it's kiss the one goodbye (for tonight) to welcome back
the prodigal daughter? Well, we got dinner on Friday to see
where this lands
cursing, not for the first, the over-activeness of these here
glands
forcing myself to rationalize, or at least understand

but what the hell, I'll never tell, what'll happen next
with me an' (maybe) my michelle.

Weaving

In an enclosed, grimy,
Somewhat worn
corner of Tsim Sha Tsui, the U.N. of Kowloon,
We await,
Second floor of the Mirador,
(second only to the Chunking, the infamous
hub of the developing world
into the Chinese Empire).

The ineptly-named mansions,
With giant pastel hands for chairs;
Dax, dark-hair-pieces and brightly-festooned boxes
Of plantain fufu for sale
On the glass shelves.

A ritual emerges,
Spun by Marie, the Togolese woman, curved and
statuesque,
Whose skin shimmers,
Oil spill in the summer heat

As she unwinds bredren's frayed locks
with the patience of an artisan
In Afro-French flavoured syllables,
murmurs pleasantries and inquiries

Begins to reform sleek rows of
Disciplined jet lattices
On his crown.

Smoked Pearl

As I lounge and immerse myself
With the lyrical lushness of Lauryn Hill,
On the screen overhead, conversations around peppered
with
piquant Akan, deep Ewe, peppery pidgin with the necessary
English.

A tiny hair shop, hidden from view,
As disparate black-and-brown strands
Are embraced by skilful hands
And re-shaped, an elegant tapestry
Through an art of weaving ...

At Nights...

Careening back
968 express to Yuen Long
in the deep black of the tropical dampness
Saw a girl who looked just like her
Straight mane like a midnight waterfall
with streaks of fury sweet and glorious
Slim elegant honey clad simply
C-girl dark shirt new jeans

Rapid fire smoky pitch
to her sharp-edged canto-chatter
on her shiny videoIpodmobile
Maybe a week old

The rest didn't exist apparently
Except her own virtual reality

And it reminded me of her
just like her
Livin' gorgeous in her own youthful insanity

At nights, now
Pondering wondering
Whatever it is, to woo her back
from across the widening void
of our disparity,
my stubbornness, her vanity

Smoked Pearl

finally, sent in
black-and-white
on an electric ice neon blue screen
a few simple
plastic clicks
my plea

waiting, breathless, in silence.

The Last Frontier

The websites
Proliferate, viruses of the mind
Buzzing furiously
Penetrating their intended targets

With a few, well-chosen
Catalysts
Words on the screen

Exciting that
Raw, atavistic impulse
Throbbing raw and livid
Beneath the
Antiseptic script

Immigration, race, IQ, crime

Fluid as toxin

Breeding response
Blogs, comments, posts, rebuttals
Awash in fear and rage

Smoked Pearl

Surfing, blindly, at first

Negotiating electronic waves
Sweeping cyberspace
To a chilling crescendo

Within seeming chaos

Even the raw, undulating moans
The gleaming flesh
On sale, on other sites

Reiterate the visceral message
To the quasi-cerebral quarrel

Of who retains dominance

No power relinquished
Without struggle

Even here, on the bright wide screens
Of the last frontier

For Sister Rita Dove

*A poem for former US Poet Laureate Rita Dove, who came
to share her verse and her life at the University of Hong
Kong on 17 October 2006. Sister, this is for you, with
warmest regards.*

crown of lustrous crinkles
exuded a soothing warmth
as her elegant sinuous, slightly
sibilant words samba'd above,
through the spaces between the sere walls
of the lecture hall,
waltzing tales of empires and libraries,
merengues of bloodshed on cut cane, shredded sprigs of
parsley,
and an intense tango between an incensed bus driver,
and a quiet seamstress who refused to submit,
on a day not so long ago, in Montgomery, Alabama.

The crowd was rapt in the motions of her fluttering fabric,
especially us three, an unknown sister, Nyaka and me,
as she recalled the stumbles, the crashes, stubbed toes, tired
steps,
onerous hours, lost sleep, grit, sweat and pain that devoured
large slices
of life itself, to recreate
the effortless flow and leap and step and sway and laugh
for joy to keep from cryin'
mesmeric patterns of her lyrical dance.

For Yupha

I still remember the taste of her mouth,
upon mine, for hours on end, as if the dampblack night
on the lip of the Gulf would never pass,
tender, moist hibiscus was her embrace,
but a blossom that would wilt, and never again see light.

Hours later, she was gone, as was I,

after five days
that was another lifetime.

Waking up once more into the cloying mist and smog
which is now existence,
I still have to believe there is a sunrise.

Star 1

I would love you
with the force of a dying sun,
our union the harbinger
of a glorious dawn,
through both the grim broil
and soothing bask of the voluminous daylight,

Which will cease, only after the last embers
have burnt, stardust and silence,
into the vastness of the beyond.

Would it be so,
but I am bound, spiralling a solitary fury
in the utter blackness of the heavens,
while thine eyes flicker for a moment,
upon I, the tail spark of a raging comet,

and rest, solitude calm,
upon the jewel'd tapestry afloat,
them, the less distant luminaries
of the Southern Sky.

Deportee

twenty minutes too late at home
crowded, with nine others
just as teak-brown, was the difference

between scrubbing floors bare of dirt
and a cell alive with its stench.

Stomachs clench
for those who have outstayed their usefulness.

Nothing we can say, for
bitter reward for eleven years' service,

not one day,
that counted towards
any permanent stay.

When they finally release her, it will
be a bitter homecoming indeed.

The two hundred every once a week for me
was a cleaner house.

For the four children, education, now stripped, futures
mired back into frustration,

The platitude of the benign employer
was that she was cheerful, oh so dependable

but the Hong Kong government, in their infinite
officialdom
with charts and tables, and precise social value apparently
in mind
deemed them all expendable.

Festivals of Autumn

The bower encloses
faded porcelain tiles scuffed

by the passage of multitudes of shoes

small, large, broad, narrow tiny and all between

under the serene stare
the benevolent Amida deep in solitary contemplation

but this afternoon awoke with samba riot garland parade,
elegantly crafted, matsuri ornate, overhead

crowded, overwhelmed with the bright pastel and candy-
hued beauty

of children's lanterns, fluttering and swaying to the
whirring electric gale of the steel fans

charcoal ink was slashed intricately into riddles that
brushed
gently over charcoal smooth little heads, as they

rushed and giggled
puzzled and quibbled

eyes bright as lunar glow, cheeky grins richer an' sweeter
than lotus paste
the moon tonight indeed may be

at its most silvery resplendent

Smoked Pearl

but it will pale
besides the pure restless illumination of they, the

multi-coloured lanterns on display, mingling and laughing
with the
raucous, joyous indescribable tableau of children at play

Pickton^{viii}

not for sale, anymore
but the bodies, swaying and full haunt me
every time I set eyes upon full gloss
of the photographs, wailing sirens in the background;

once, they must have had that late-night allure,

but something more powerful seduced them,
slowly, through the blood, maws, noses and veins

'til it wizened them, hardened them, blinded them,
bodies full of every poison known to hell

'til they agreed en masse to be bought wholesale

so pickton, with knowledge of hams, and ribs, rashers, ears,
snouts, tongues and picnic shoulders tore

into them with a savage hunger where

the last preservation of the women on display

was not in a red-light smeared window,
crumbling city block,
darkened night club

but in a freezer, in odds and ends,
with the other cuts of meat
to be consumed in a ghoulish buffet.

Rugby Sevens

A beautiful and skilful barbarity, on and off the thundering
field, on this noblest of
Hong Kong Central weekends,

a multi-regimented prize-fight

where titans sweep and weave on the field,
multi-hued as the stripes on their rippled backs battling
swift rounds

with one brown oblong orb flying desperately within

to the roar of generally rose-faced crowds, heightened by
costumed antics, copious jugs of Carlsberg, Pimm's No. 1
Cup and Heineken

just as adept, in rows and sections, neat, clear and complete

in maintaining the order of standings, from flags aloft and
wild cheers,

to a stony gaze, a silent shake, a curled lip, an almost
imperceptible sneer

should one wish to sneak a reserved chair

upright or on thrones, it's still boozy, merriment everywhere

raven-haired girls smiling into blue eyes while breezy
blondes and brunettes barely clad as nurses, maids and
divas gyrate drunkenly in the stands with the vikings,
pirates, and captains of industry to the seductive rhythms of
the large screens

Smoked Pearl

Take care not to listen too closely to the whispers of grave-
faced, grey-locked men, who with every sip, dry chuckle,
and occasional glance at the field
trade China, Hong Kong, Sri Lanka and several of the other
nations on board.

While their stalwarts battle on the field for paltry hours, old
men in corporate boxes receive the truest prize.

Outside, another match commences, as crowds thrust and
pass and feint and wheel to gain access, to gain entrance to
the golden goals

some will be New Zealand's, others Korea's
England's numerous will draw at best, to the triumph of a
very few Samoa's, not to mention the valiant if doomed
efforts of Sri Lanka's, Hong Kong's and China's
to gain mastery of the fight of season

strength and fame without fairness or shame

Welcome to the Rugby Sevens – love, wealth and war
where the mighty flourish and the desirous look on from
afar
far outside the hallowed gates of Hong Kong Stadium,

the weekend is busy, the weather is fair,
local masses mill at malls, to shop and eat and display their
various wares,
few know of the glorious battle,

and very few have been taught to care.

Words on a Page
3 November 2006

first time I remember climbing the stage

was when words were alive
and spoken lyrics the rage

cacophony of flows high-jivin' and intertwinin'

angular words, cutting airs, razor wit
moist, chewy syllables so rich, so filling
they coulda been Duncan Hines, not Duncan's lines

trying to slice and sweeten the elastic phrases that sought to
stretch and expand

the sycophantic cadence of the background band

laughin', cryin', livin', hustlin', lovin', dyin',
reprisin' life in voluminous webs
through the patterns of glowsilver aquaneon frayed denim

tattered copies in back pockets with the bags of rough hemp
slung on backs
that silhouetted the crowd through the smoke-lit richness
of the endless evening
but those endless nights became
faded etches, some went obscure, others sought fame
or a different name

a cosmic click, brush or rub
Delete, or Alt, revised the mainframe

Smoked Pearl

towards a calmer day, more sedate consumption
amidst quiet murmurs, Brie slices and Chardonnay

Where the full-blown new jack swingers of verbs
thigh deep in amorous nouns
with fresh adjectives on display

eventually tamed their wicked ways

living within margins
to become words on a page.

Wasted Days

Wasted days a long-drawn
burn against a life
a candle, once magnificent, smooth,
whose flame has tapered down to a
swollen stub, waxen tears and puddles
that disfigure its former beauty –
the light, the promise.

An old candle now, that placed a wick
another end, in youthful arrogance
a double blade of fire, that scorches
twice as bright, and extinguishes
thrice as fast

at last, upon an early demise
realize, that others will not recognize
the glory of the blaze
the briefness of the fame

but the last flicker of the blackened stump
molten translucence of the swimming wax
that never had a name

Waif of Honour

Morning cobalt mist's deep heavy grit was a cloak of
lingering somnolence upon the still figure in the tiny room,
reluctant, today, to lift its ponderous self to the heavens,
drawn to the soft, sweet melancholy of
cinnamon and earth, blood and demerara, palest of ambers,
deepest of teaks in a face shrouded by the pillow.

A spread of silk strands from her crown so jet in their
magnificence,
That they emit their own shampoo commercial
luminescence greet me, as I struggle awake, stumble into
the steaming shower, scrape and rub and tuck and
Tidy myself into existence, a groom for the still dark world
    to embrace

But not without a glance, a quiet kneel, lips on hidden
    cheek for the waif who
Rises and livens by the rays of the solar prince, a guest at
the wedding of man and cracked chattering street cobbles,
whose bouquet blooms only when the rite is done,
An unknown sun, for whom even the bride, ever-hissing
and impatient waits,
As she peers into the chamber, with the solemn mist, at the
reluctant beauty,
of her waif of honour.

On the Death of Young Men
A dirge for Heath, Brad, and other victims of the plague

The morning of January the 22nd, Greenwich Village time.
A swallow, a whisper, an atrophied vein,
Was enough to send him back to where all once came,
from a celluloid void to a brief screen memory, deep into
    the night,
crowded amidst the garish infomercials, quaint outline of a
    winning tragic grace.

But they said he was beautiful.

Remember River Phoenix? Who does, these days of wars,
bomb blasts, melting markets, swelling oceans, drying
fields, swarming migrants and writers' strikes,
pitched battles, bitter campaigns in the heartland for a
    world divided.

But they said he was beautiful, too.

Even unto Death, whose feathers stroked his crown as he
lay, nightlife tarmac and streams of burning crystal binding
    him,
for a last heady embrace.

Incandescent were his blank eyes, glorious was his lifeless
    face,
But the world turns relentless: new, aspiring sparks succeed
    the ashes, take their place,
these who shine brightest, nourish their glow,
through mask'd fears, adulation, liquid courage, dunes of
    chemical flow.

Smoked Pearl

Our quotidian demises may be more mundane,
Crashed cars, scarred lungs, seized hearts, or the gradual rot
Of a once-plump frame,

Never mind the absence of a brief, glitter fortune,
or the flicker of an un-eternal fame.
Regardless, years from now, someone will still recall his
        name,

For they said he was beautiful.

Immigration

a deep and abiding anger
resonates through two clear, scratched inches
of plexiglass,

suffuses through the tinny echoes of the stentorian
 announcement
that presumes authoritative calm amidst the steady
 cacophony of at least
five distinct languages shoving and bustling through the
 crowded foyer
with painstakingly thorough regard for race, creed, title and
 class

and, for us, this comes to a gradual, intense simmer, over

four hours, awaiting a single swift chop on stark bleach and
 ink forms –

three identical documents, required to be so complete and
ordered in their purity that even a misplaced indentation
could be the subject of weeks' more further review.

Two sets of bespectacled worthies, clad in her ex-Majesty's
faded blues, with less-compassionate stares and very
 different shoes,
give stern yet fraternal advice, reassurances of due process and
swift completion, at the last to be undercut by the gravelly
threats   of

a single five-foot bulldog of a beldam, who without a single
glance at me, the one with the passport of privilege (for a world
that is a string of fortresses rather than a global village), snarled
out her final decision: a last review, a last reprieve, then stomped
off triumphantly, documents lying still in the clear plastic
sleeve–

Smoked Pearl

Final sentence; Seven days extension, but at a Pyrrhic cost,
as I glanced at the olive-tan cheeks of my beloved turned wan,
the chocolate drop eyes lashed bleeding teary lymph at the
    effort
of supplication. But she was fortunate. There were others, in
    the same room
same raven-gloss tresses spilling down their backs, earth tones of
    various shades
similar animated lilt in their conversation, at the end of fourteen
days faced imminent repatriation

As we left, brief achievement soured rapidly into
    recrimination, rancour
dangerously alluring, as I wondered at the tireless
    determination
of how Asia's world city zealously practices immigration.

Smoked Pearl

Emergency Call, Response
Avian flu scare, 2008

Call

They feel
barbs,
blood-sponged and quivering
slippery-soft white-and-flesh
tendrils of swollen tonsils

some will endure only
a brief rawness, mild scarlet irritation
but where the grip of the vice is more…
insistence observes
an altered permutation, gasping
for breath, for a daylight's flutter,
welcoming the extreme
cleanse of concentrate radiation

It expands, ink-like city-wide
under the hue of mist
that smears over the sights…

Smoked Pearl

Response

So? Mask up, be still,
lay alone, be chill
we wouldn't want to give
our foreign guests a fright

We've closed schools,
taken precautions
to keep this our own private blight

endure the claws
and forgive us our
usual dearth of prescience passing for sight
Or the malady
that we presently brave
will seem gentle, ever so slight...

Deep Cool

I return to the deep cool, that sweet chilled breeze that
wafts downwards from the meadow of ashen blossoms
overhead, rich in soot, perspiration and ardour. It is early on
a Friday, where well-worn tires begin to churn, glossy
leather and torn rubber begin to slap and clop onto the split
sidewalks, but it is gradual, almost sedate, a procession
rather than explosion, immersing the mind in a muted
parade of simultaneous souls and solitude—a group of
seniors by a Lego-bright jungle gym,

intensely focused on the graceful, disciplined arcs and
flourishes of *tai chi*, each movement closely and
deliberately executed to the strains of a recorded *erhu*
wailing its well-timed discord from a nearby boom-box,
others sitting on benches or planter edges, engaged in a
life's contemplation, with whatever hours or days or months
they may or may not have remaining on this orb. The
tropical sun, a scorching union between a topaz and a blood
orange, has yet to gently roast the gray billows in the sky
into cloying steam, the steel crush of vehicles that choke
the arteries of North Kowloon from mid-morning until the
ink-blackness of late evening, has yet to appear, so the few
students that appear on the streets, alone or with friends or
Mummy, or a creaking Grandma or a stoic teak-hued
Filipina or Indonesian helper doubling as pack mule for a
privileged child, starch whites, muted blues, crisp shirts are
able to complete their journey in silence.

Smoked Pearl

I follow
this inner pilgrimage to a spilling of the serene that bathes
and cleanses and gently clears the grit of a hundred days,
washing the soil to a distant lagoon past the temporal.
Then, a last gasp, a final splash just before the office gate.
Then I emerge slowly, reluctantly, but with hard eyes,
prepared for the first of many bricks, scrapes, cuts and
barbs of the day. At best, the respite is but a balm that will
scorch as much as it now soothes.

11 April 2008

Beautiful Tomorrows
After a little Marvin Gaye...

Curious I enjoy
A sharp bittersweet
On nights like this
Overcast, but not yet swollen-damp

Muggy and breezy chill by swirls
Of a giant rinse cycle overhead

What spins in my ears, live-an'-youtube direct
Digital crisp, with stunning plasma clarity
are

The first keen notes of a falsetto sad tomorrow

As Marvin flies high in a friendly melting sky

But as a child I never quite understood why

As mahogany an' sepia tears from an amberviolet voice

Wash over the reverent screen

The brother gloriously preens with ever so delicious a
sheen
Of defiance at tragedy he moulds exquisite

For a yesterday I was too little then to comprehend

Last blip, final chord, clip's end

Smoked Pearl

And, as ashen storms settle for the night,

I click replay on the mouse

To explore

What other emotions I may rend.

May Days for June the Fourth

ask not for whom the blood flows
with the waters,
cold and clear as lymph, as the mortal stain widens,
it flows for we,
blossoms through cracked stone,
gongs and wails clanging
monotone elegies
amidst sodden, crumbled hills
already suspects are being questioned...
cinder block crumbs, for impersonating brick
fence wire frames that masqueraded as steel
but it is their very weakness that brings forth trickles,
human miracles, from the deep
but will not rouse the youngest from their sudden sleep

even now, as grief from the core of the land wells gushes
over its fragments, people bind fists, tears, hammers, flesh
and earth as only a family bereaved can; to stand, toil and
stay alive

survive, and even demand a justice that may forthcome
under the light of a flame, empathy or shame

unlike the events nineteen years before to this day
but who can say,
when shock subsides?

Meanwhile in Rangoon

In the bay of a Bengal tiger that shrieked its silvery spume
of fury over tarnished pagodas
shredded petals cling to delta silt
amidst drowned palm fronds

but there is final victory here.
a unanimous decision! a new constitution!
men in aviator glasses and olive khaki
ever ready to defend the motherland thank
the outside world for their support, but are insistent
on handling the tedium of the necessary tasks
that may prove too onerous for those from Western
        institutions

in the monsoon heat, far from their perfectly chilled
        corridors,
the air is enriched by the reek of putrefaction, but not just
from blemished sacks on crumbling docks, grotesque bloat
of human, beast and corpse or the wreaths of bottle-green
flies that greet such bounty with elation, but the white,
        sharp smiles
behind the shades that beam enormous satisfaction.

Crackle[ix]
13 - 15 September 2006

Crackles of a lonely on-line hate
finally burst harsh and livid
onto the every day bustle.

I couldn't believe it was Canada anymore,
crashing bodies, wails of dismay
on the swimming cobbles of the cafeteria

She lies, eternal shock from
the smash of steel fists that stole
hope.

Near another two score lie in agony,
incomprehension;
a site of sustenance a near-turned mausoleum

two photos struck with equal 9mm intensity
she, the eighteen-year-old dark-eyed beauty,
crowned in mortarboard and jangling earring glory
who will never see such wonder down here again

he, already shrouded in death and pain, posing
falcon's pitiless glare
with his weapons of mass obliteration

as clicks and crackles slowly unravel
on a mute screen
to falteringly explain, in bits and bytes

what should never have been.

Watery Sieves

Blinding splitting fluorescent and sapphire electric
    whitesmash
Sears the panorama into bewilderment
A singular sonic scream sharp stab pierce the huddled
melancholy of the darkened heavens, and then
In fits and blubbers, begins to weep again, drains swollen,
heavy clay and deep loam moistening under the steel
supports of the sleek gleam of aqua drenched tinted glass,
height titanic, office heights supple as sharkskin.
Public housing estates, moulded at an industrial pace and
hued an industrial puce, may be less fortunate.

T-shirts for Obama

after the latest

on-screen euphoria

I decided to sport
My newly minted
(but meticulously designed)
conviction,
stamped red and white and cream
on a field of navy blue
at ease with its near-blackness

strolled out into the brash glitter of Kowloon nightlife
where throngs of passersby
flicked on, flicked off
flooded by
teems and masses wailing

babbles of voices
mobile phones, headphones, fake watches and glasses
Conversed feet, arms, necks and Gucci-clad asses

Stepped onto Sai Yee through Argyle
Where the t-shirts racked out on night display seemed
quizzical, but indifferent
Mao, Bob Marley, Che, Lennon, Diesel, and various
bathing apes staring curiously
At the graven tenacity of the newest, if solitary celebrity

Smoked Pearl

They know will, given time,
Like the rest woven in cheap vivid hues
Bleed pearls, blood and indigo
Into the inevitable wash
Of faded figures

But there were nods, winks and silent affirmation
Stall to stall, light to light
And it seemed there might soon be a new hero
To regale the night, four for a hundred dollars Hong Kong.

I was wrong.

At Tsim Sha Tsui,
The dream ended
The moment the throngs parted.

And the telescopic lense armed hordes
Emerged, confident to discover

One, large, placid, mildly grey tourist
Plodding directly ahead

Lifted his wrinkled eyelids
Slightly aloft

With a cold aquamarine stare

As if at an unwanted ware

And what became clear

Was the difficulty

In an actual sale.

Mother and Child

As the voluminous serpent of the
Sheung Wan /Island line
skated its steel slither
past the crush of Admiralty,
throngs of Wanchai,
mobs of Causeway Bay towards
the quieter groves of Central Library, Tin Hau branch

I finally saw something good tonight.

Previous stop,
Diminutive mother, seraph son, amidst the sullen, retiring
    mass
squeezed, last mice into an overflowing maw when
The jaw-like doors snapped,
Right at their heads
She took instant, feral fright

But in that moment of near-mastication
She gained much more than that.

With a rare serene grace,
She withdrew, regained a now-empty
place underneath the station's fluorescent light
And, as the serpent began to career away,
In search of a more satisfying bite,

A last glance
had mother in immutable calm,
Holding her wide-eyed lad,
Ever so tight.

8 October 2008

Enlighten

It is three forty, near the end
of a muted evening, where the
tarnished silver light of the
moon is blurred by the remains
of the night's smog, but the
innumerable shards of Kowloon City's neon crystal
        are all ...

It is three-forty, near the end
of a muted evening. The nightfall smog blurs a moon
the colour of tarnished silverware.
The innumerable shards of Kowloon City's neon crystal are
all

riven

on the slim, crumpled, supine
unconsciously restful feline form
of my darling.

Lids and lips shut against the windows' glare,
its piercing scrutiny.

She is aswirl from the gravity of her dreams,
a twitch, shrug or rustle aloft
sparks in a struggle to escape their undertow

six ten has arrived, diamond stare broadens gradually
        to a golden beam
that will not redeem lost hours, days, stretches of time upon
        end
where all hues of light supervise her toil, sun/star/sign
        incandescence.

Smoked Pearl

Fluorescence off aluminum foil,
becoming embroiled
under the blistering lights.

The next false dawn
she returns from her labours
when darkness almost ceased, almost pleased to earn a
    meagre keep
then blink her lids to snare a scrap or shred of sleep.

I myself alight, as my worry smoulders,
at the sight of grinning lips and sagging shoulders
then bursts aflame out of pure fright

that my darling will begin to drift between night and day
just to say her effort earns her way, then plummet into
a deeper slumber, and drift away.

I'd rather see her another night, another day,
Another night where she rests undisturbed, unafraid
let only the neon signs burn and slave,
and release her dreams to delight in play.

29 October, 2008

All Had Dreams
Five years after the start of the Iraq War...

All had dreams
that revealed themselves to us in streams
over burning sand, still scorched from shells,
spent, gasping bitter cordite coated with benzene.

All had dreams
that relieve themselves in crimson streams,
over the blackened ruins, hissing
metal, sizzling rubber, weeping gasoline.

All had dreams
that relied on electronic streams,
through now-molten wires, crackling,
sound gnaws, screen jaws, talking head squeals
from a plethora of e-zines.

All had dreams
emanating from an unseen,
irreverence at the pulpit,
mullahs roaring at the *fellaheen.*

Now only a few have dreams
sputtering from between
the rehearsed lines that wed black gold and death,
as poppies flourish and multiply,
nourished by growing streams.

Swing States
21 October 2008

It's the last chapter
of the supersaga of
America's latest undeclared war (not Iran, or Pakistan, nor
    Syria or Bob Barr)

Unhindered by 4000 stainless steel coffins in the desert
(conversion rate US GI 1 = 250 Iraqi/Afghans)
Flooded levees, swirl-shattered homes;
Splintered by submerged cars, winds of the gods gone wild,
Alive with rumours from the stars;

Heedless of the colossal corpses of that lovely couple,
Freddie Mac and Fannie Mae, that consumed (to their
    demise)
Most of them remaining houses left from that man an'
    nature fray.

Unimportant, really, look what the pundits brought today!
Salvos flying fiercer, elephant ears in full flower
from a sweet young breeze up north
that has them talking trash about Yo'bama;
The other old guy just watchin', Biden his time.

Now may McCain, maybe McCain't, but now he's Palin
Behind his Betty Crocker with a bull-moose blastin'
    automatic
That has all'a them good ol' red-state flatland boys hollerin'
    ecstatic.

Neck and neck between a donkey and a honkey,
Out with charismatic, don't need Harvard school-boy
    pedantic
Book-bannin', pistol packin' Palin's on the scene.

Smoked Pearl

One week green, never mind America the free!
By God, we need the autocratic,
To bless the land, bless the wars, and punish evildoers for
    their heresies
the Bible just done got re-wrote, and rewarded the
    Pharisees,
But dear jackasses and jennies of the other party,
Please don't panic....

Give a week in the maelstrom of Yankee politics,
Where polls and surveys are going manic,

A forthright, earnest tongue'll slip when it clicks into
    automatic

And even Karl Rove, Grandmaster of the below-the-
    Beltway shuffle
will descend into the frantic.
Which was, six weeks later, quite prophetic

Tina Fey channeled Caribou Barbie right across the Bering
    Strait
but only Saturday Night Live and maybe Putin (or whoever
    he put in)
were pleased.

The small matter of a global economic meltdown
still brought the great elephant to its aged knees

And the last I heard before I clicked the channel
was a rant, a bellow and a raspy wheeze
of a pachyderm trying to convince the crowd
of poisonous acorns, and socialism in the breeze
How Rezko, Rev. Wright, Ayers and others we don't know
are still major political players, symptoms of an un-
American disease ....

Smoked Pearl

Well naysayers, it ain't quite over until the fat jumbo sings
So as Ohio and Florida, Missouri, Virginia, Nevada, North
Carolina and even Indiana continue to flutter flip-flop with
every blow in the ring
Keep on chanting, "Swing, swing states, swing!"

Tonight (on the Victory of Obama)
5 November 2008

Come here, my child, and listen,
I wanna tell you, kid,
There is no can't;
'cause tonight we did.
By refusing to continue
as we have been bid,
these last, few troubled, difficult years.

From here, our mission will be to heal division
and make restitution to the empire of possibilities we have
　　freed
from the maelstrom unleashed by thoughtlessness and
greed

Make a vow to strive, to succeed, to seek opportunity
and not dwell on our need, not just wishing
that change may come somehow, someway.

My dear, change has been achieved this very day
So, I don't wanna hear
that you couldn't, you wouldn't, can't be bothered, or maybe
　　you shouldn't,
That you're not the captain of your soul, but a slave to your
　　id
Don't tell me you didn't, for tonight we did

Smoked Pearl

Make no mistake, in a day, a year, even a lifetime
We may never be rid of violence, hatred, conflict, or
    poverty
Suffering, uncaring, shallowness or hypocrisy

But never render hardship as an excuse
or use inability as a convenient fib
I said some time ago, Yes We Can

And tonight, Oh Yes We Did.

Woke from Wake

In those final moments
Just before the brain snaps into
Full consciousness
To endure, as paranoia wells through the cracks
The glare, gloom, glamour glassiness of the ripening day,

Morning rest is a snug cotton paradise
Set aglow by the shimmer of cut glass sparkles on the pane

Entwined with my darling and I
To the gentle cadence of deep chest breathing
Vacuum, soothe, smooth, vacuum, soothe, smooth

Until the reluctant burden of first eyelid
Wrenches its way aloft, followed by the slink of its partner,
paring open in bitter reproach

Cracked, they moisten to the reality of the dawn

Sentries alert for the inevitable assault
Upon deadened senses

But for slivers of precious seconds

The light that emanates over the approaching horizon
Blazes an entire universe prism clear

And blast!

We are
awake.

10 December 2008

Here...

Hers is a painfully exquisite tenderness that contours to my upper body with each gust and puff we emanate, sometimes in tandem in the tiniest hours of the morning, silent and sable, sprawled side by side, submerged just below the faintly rippled surface of slumber we dived in earlier, immersed ourselves in the rituals of its silvery, murky reaches, struggled with hidden frustrations, seemingly fantastical aspirations, philosophical confusions, then glided onwards to a bizarre array of coloured thoughts and metaphysical contusions. I swim unafraid, knowing I can always ascend sharply, cleave the fluid layer between the chill of actuality and the wonders of the deep, and she will still be there, large soft lids submerged in their own pools of inner fantasy, lotion hardened to the sweetness of nougat on her face that crackles with every breath and flare, limbs curled around a third pillow, and an eerie, pleasing glow washed over the perfumed strands of her raven hair. We are here.

11 February 2009

CR

Advance responses to "Smoked Pearl: Poems of Hong Kong and Beyond", by Akin Jeje (Akinsola Olufemi Jeje).

Smoked Pearl was a semi-finalist for the inaugural international Proverse Prize in 2009. Publication supported by Hong Kong Arts Development Council.

"A fine collection of free verse; exuberant and thoughtful. Serious, thoughtful and moral; angry, but also loving and compassionate." — Proverse Prize Judges.

"Jeje sees the gleam revealed within the grime: his titular smoked pearl evocative of this interplay of light and dark. For tarnished things must once have been precious, and though Jeje writes of wasted days, he recognises the briefness, 'the glory of the blaze.' ... But for all that Jeje sees — the injustice, the silence and the blame — these darknesses of the human soul are not total: the night ends, hope dawns." — Viki Holmes, author of *miss moon's class.*

"Jeje's gaze swivels from the intensely private to the trans-continentally public, but he remains ever a self-confessed "jack swinger of verbs," offering us luscious, "amorous nouns." Lustillusion. Despairconfusion. This profusion of sights and sounds is tender, scintillating, thought provoking. Priceless." — Xu Xi, author of *Habit of a Foreign Sky* and *Evanescent Isles.*

"Richly imaginative. ... *Smoked Pearl* has a vivid personal touch, characteristically descriptive of the poet's experience and sensations of Hong Kong and beyond his life in this city." — Yeeshan Yang, author of *Whispers and Moans* and *Palma's Tears.*

About the Author

Canadian poet **Akin Jeje** lives in Hong Kong. An active poet and spoken-word performer, Jeje's works have been published and featured in both Canada and Hong Kong. Jeje's first work, *Dreaming of The Sands* was published in Canada in 1999. His first full-length poetry collection, *Smoked Pearl: Poems of Hong Kong and Beyond* was a semi-finalist for the 2009 International Proverse Prize, and published by Proverse Hong Kong in 2010.

Jeje's work was also featured in the collaborative poem *A poem for Jack Layton, by 14 Canadian Poets,* published in Canada's The Globe and Mail newspaper, August 26, 2011, and his most recent publication was in Hong Kong's 2014 *Poetry Outloud Too* anthology. Jeje has also published in other Hong Kong and Canadian publications such as *fifty-fifty, Asian Cha, Carousel,* and *Filling Station.*

Jeje is a regular performer at Hong Kong's monthly *Poetry Outloud* event, and has been for almost a decade. In addition, Jeje served as the MC for Hong Kong's *Peel Street Poets* collective from 2007 to 2014, and is still a regular participant. In addition, Jeje is also an advisor to the Hong Kong International Young Readers' Festival, and has been a volunteer moderator for the Hong Kong International Festival from 2012 to the present. Jeje's community participation includes performing his poetry for public events and in schools, and has been presenting education seminars on poetry for secondary schools since 2014.

Notes

[i] "i" is deliberate. By the use of a small "i", Jeje suggests that separation from "Mama" causes a reduction of himself.

[ii] Caleb Jordan was a twenty-one year old young man who used to be a member of a congregation that Jeje attended. Caleb Johnson died in his sleep when he was away studying. Jeje wrote, "I heard about this when I attended my first service there. He was American, but he grew up in Hong Kong, and was much beloved by his peers and elders."

In this poem also, "i" is used for "I". The context suggests that the rationale is similar to that in "Mama" (see above).

[iii] "One, questioning if questions, thoughts, ideas would ever be allowed,

to be as galaxial as the conquest of space."

Asked about the use of the comma after the word, "allowed" (unusual in a structure like this), Jeje noted as follows: "The comma halts the natural flow of the sentence, in the same way that a totalitarian regime halts the free flow of information or speech. A subtle, unusual device, but it underlines the general point I make in the theme."

[iv] One thousand eves is three years. Five thousand is fifteen years, as long as I'd had vices up to that point.

[v] On Boxing Day, 26 December 2005, a shootout between two black youth gangs on Toronto's Yonge Street resulted in the death of Jane Creba, a 15-year-old white student who had been shopping with her family. Six other bystanders – four men and two women – were wounded. The incident took place on one of Toronto's most crowded streets, just a few blocks north of the Toronto Eaton Centre, on that very busy shopping day. This made international headlines. What did not make international headlines, however, is that numerous black youths and civilians had also been killed and injured by the same senseless wave of violence that had been plaguing Toronto's black community for some time,

but there was little outcry…until someone considered to be a mainstream Canadian died.
"A rudebwai" = A rude boy (Rude boy, rudeboy, rudie, rudi or rudy are common terms used in Jamaica). In the 1960s they were also used for juvenile delinquents and criminals in Jamaica, and have since been used in other contexts. In the United Kingdom in the 2000s, the terms "rude boy" and "rude girl" have become slang which mainly refer to people (largely youths) who are involved in street culture, similar to "gangsta" or "badman".

Therefore, the phrase, "a rudebwai 'pan a mike", translates to "a rude boy upon a microphone", which refers, in this context, to a young streetwise dancehall reggae or hip hop musician rhyming or singing via the microphone.
"T.O." – "Toronto".
[vi] "A moment's slip –": The dash is used here in order to emphasize the occurrence of a singular moment where control was lost, and the source of the accident.
[vii] An allusion to the Greek myth. This reference also touches on the outcome of the 1994 African-American film starring Allen Payne and Jada Pinkett Smith.

The Greek hero, Jason had been advised that he and his Argonauts would never arrive home safely after the successful quest for the Golden Fleece, without enlisting the aid of Orpheus, as they had to pass the islands where the Sirens lived, who sang bewitching songs, luring sailors to destruction on their rocky shores. So, as they passed the Sirens' shores, Orpheus played on his lyre. The song was so beautiful, loud and powerful, that it drowned out the Sirens' songs. The song was referred to thereafter as "Jason's Lyric".
[viii] Robert William "Willie" Pickton (born 26 October 1949) of Port Coquitlam, British Columbia, Canada is a former pig farmer and serial killer convicted of the second-degree murders of six women. He is also charged in the deaths of an additional twenty women, many of them prostitutes and

drug users from Vancouver's Downtown Eastside. In December 2007 he was sentenced to life in prison, with no possibility of parole for 25 years – the longest sentence available under Canadian law for murder. During the trial's first day of jury evidence, 22 January 2007, the Crown stated he confessed to forty-nine murders to an undercover police officer posing as a cellmate. The Crown reported that Pickton told the officer that he wanted to kill another woman to make it an even 50, and that he was caught because he was "sloppy". (*Wikipedia*)

[ix] This poem commemorates the Dawson College shootings on 13 September 2006, where a gunman killed one student and injured nineteen others. Sadly, it followed the all-too-frequent pattern of a deranged young man literally blazing out his anger on innocents.

ABOUT PROVERSE HONG KONG

Proverse Hong Kong is based in Hong Kong with long-term and expanding regional and international connections.

Proverse has published novels, novellas, fictionalized autobiography, non-fiction (including autobiography, biography, history, memoirs, sport, travel narratives), single-author poetry collections, children's, teens / young adult and academic books. Other interests include diaries, and academic works in the humanities, social sciences, cultural studies, linguistics and education. Some Proverse books have accompanying audio texts. Some are translated into Chinese.

Proverse welcomes authors who have a story to tell, wisdom, perceptions or information to convey, a person they want to memorialize, a neglect they want to remedy, a record they want to correct, a strong interest that they want to share, skills they want to teach, and who consciously seek to make a contribution to society in an informative, interesting and well-written way. Proverse works with texts by non-native-speaker writers of English as well as by native English-speaking writers.

The name, "Proverse", combines the words "prose" and "verse" and is pronounced accordingly.

THE PROVERSE PRIZE

The Proverse Prize, an annual international competition for an unpublished book-length work of fiction, non-fiction, or poetry, was established in January 2008. It is open to all who are at least eighteen on the date they sign the entry form. Unusually for a competition of this nature, there is no restriction based on nationality, residence or citizenship.

The objectives of the Proverse Prize are: to encourage excellence and / or excellence and usefulness in publishable written work in the English Language, which can, in varying degrees, "delight and instruct". Entries are invited from anywhere in the world. Semi-finalists to date include writers born, resident, or who have been resident in Andorra, Australia, Canada, Germany, Hong Kong, New Zealand, Nigeria, Singapore, South Africa, Taiwan, The Bahamas, the Peoples' Republic of China, the United Arab Emirates, the United

Kingdom, the USA.
FOUNDERS: Verner Bickley and Gillian Bickley. To celebrate
their lifelong love of words in all their forms as readers, writers,
editors, academics, performers, and publishers.
HONORARY LEGAL ADVISOR: Mr Raymond T. L. Tse.
HONORARY ACCOUNTANT: Mr Neville Chow.
HONORARY JUDGES: Anonymous.
HONORARY ADVISORS: Bahamian poet Marion Bethel; UK
translator, Margaret Clarke; UK linguist & lexicographer David
Crystal; Canadian poet and academic, Jonathan Hart; Swedish
linguist Björn Jernudd; Hong Kong University Librarian, Peter
Sidorko; Singapore poet Edwin Thumboo; Czech novelist & poet
Olga Walló.
HONORARY UK AGENT AND DISTRIBUTOR: Christine Penney
HONORARY ADMINISTRATORS: Proverse Hong Kong.

PROVERSE PRIZE WINNERS WHOSE BOOKS HAVE ALREADY BEEN
PUBLISHED BY PROVERSE HONG KONG

Laura Solomon, Rebecca Jane Tomasis, Gillian Jones, David
Diskin, Peter Gregoire, Sophronia Liu, Birgit Linder, James
McCarthy, Celia Claase, Philip Chatting.

Summary Terms and Conditions
(for indication only & subject to revision)

The information below is for guidance only. Please refer to the
year-specific Proverse Prize Entry Form & Terms & Conditions,
which are uploaded in April each year onto the Proverse Hong
Kong website: <www.proversepublishing.com>.
  The free Proverse E-Newsletter includes ongoing
information about the Proverse Prize. To be put on the E-
Newsletter mailing-list, email: info@proversepublishing.com
with your request.

Smoked Pearl

The Prize
1) Publication by Proverse Hong Kong, with
2) Cash prize of HKD10,000 (HKD7.80 = approx. US$1.00)

Supplementary publication grants may be made to selected other entrants for publication by Proverse Hong Kong.

Depending on the quality of the work in any year, the prize may be shared by at most two entrants or withheld, as recommended by the judges.

In 2015, the entry fee was: HKD220.00 OR GBP32.00.

Writers are eligible, who are at least eighteen on the date they sign The Proverse Prize entry documents. There is no nationality or residence restriction.

Each submitted work must be an unpublished publishable single-author work of non-fiction, fiction or poetry, the original work of the entrant, and submitted in the English language. School textbooks and plays are ineligible.

Translated work: If the work entered is a translation from a language other than English, both the original work and the translation should be previously unpublished. The submitted work will not be judged as a translation but as an original work.

Extent of the Manuscript: within the range of what is usual for the genre of the work submitted. However, it is advisable that novellas be in the range 30,000 to 45,000 words); other fiction (e.g. novels, short-story collections) and non-fiction (e.g. autobiographies, biographies, diaries, letters, memoirs, essay collections, etc.) should be in the range, 75,000 to 100,000 words. Poetry collections should be in the range, 5,000 to 25,000 words. Other word-counts and mixed-genre submissions are not ruled out.

Writers may choose, if they wish, to obtain the services of an Editor in presenting their work, and should acknowledge this help and the nature and extent of this help in the Entry Form.

KEY DATES FOR THE PROVERSE PRIZE IN ANY YEAR
(subject to confirmation and/or change)

Receipt of Entry Fees / Entry Documents	[Variable but no later than] 14 April to 31 May of the year of entry
Receipt of entered manuscripts	[From no later than] 1 May of the year of entry. Deadline: 30 June of the year of entry
Announcement of semi-finalists	July-September of the year of entry
Announcement of finalists	October-December of the year of entry
Announcement of winner/ max two winners (sharing the cash prize)	December of the year of entry to April of the year that follows the year of entry
Cash Award made	At the same time as publication of the work(s) adjudged the winner / winners of the Proverse Prize
Publication of winning work(s)	In or after November of the year that follows the year of entry

POETRY AND POETRY COLLECTIONS
Published by Proverse Hong Kong

If you have enjoyed *Smoked Pearl* by Akin Jeje, you may also enjoy the following poetry and poetry collections published by Proverse Hong Kong (all titles in English unless otherwise stated):

Astra and Sebastian, by L.W. Illsley. 2011.

Chasing light, by Patricia Glinton Meicholas. 2013.

China suite and other poems, by Gillian Bickley. 2009.

For the record and other poems of Hong Kong, by Gillian Bickley. 2003.

Frida Kahlo's Cry and Other Poems, by Laura Solomon. 2015.

Home, away, elsewhere, by Vaughan Rapatahana. 2011.

Immortelle and bhandaaraa poems,
by Lelawattee Manoo-Rahming. 2011.

In vitro, by Laura Solomon. 2nd ed. 2014.

Moving house and other poems from Hong Kong, by Gillian Bickley. 2005.

Of symbols misused, by Mary-Jane Newton. 2011.

Painting the borrowed house: poems, by Kate Rogers. 2008.

Perceptions, by Gillian Bickley. 2012.

Rain on the pacific coast, by Elbert Siu Ping Lee. 2013.

refrain, by Jason S. Polley. 2010.

Shadow play, by James Norcliffe. 2012.

Shadows in Deferment, by Birgit Bunzel Linder, 2013.

Sightings: a collection of poetry, with an essay, 'communicating poems', by Gillian Bickley. 2007.

The Layers Between, by Celia Claase (Essays and Poems), 2015.

Unlocking, by Mary-Jane Newton. 2014.

Wonder, lust & itchy feet, by Sally Dellow. 2011.

POETRY– CHINESE LANGUAGE

For the record and other poems of Hong Kong, by Gillian Bickley. Translated by Simon Chow. 2010.

Moving house and other poems from Hong Kong, translated into Chinese, with additional material, by Gillian Bickley. Edited by Tony Ming-Tak Yip. Translated by Tony Yip & others. 2008.

OTHER GENRES

We also publish in other genres, including fiction, autobiography, biography, children's illustrated books, educational books, Hong Kong educational and legal history, memoirs, teenage / young adult books, and travel. Other genres may be added.

WRITE TO US!

We are interested to read **your** response to
Akin Jeje's *Smoked Pearl: Poems of Hong Kong and Beyond*
and any other of our publications.
Please write to our email address, proverse@netvigator.com,
giving us a few sentences which you are willing for us to publish,
giving your comments on this book.
If what you write is chosen to be included
in our E-Newsletter or website,
we will select another title published by Proverse
and send you a complimentary copy.
Please include your name, email address and mailing address
when you write to us, and state whether or not we may cut or
edit your comments for publication.
We will use your initials to attribute your comments.

FIND OUT MORE ABOUT OUR AUTHORS AND BOOKS

Visit our website
http://www.proversepublishing.com

Visit our distributor's website
<www.chineseupress.com>

Follow us on Twitter
Follow news and conversation: <twitter.com/Proversebooks>
OR
Copy and paste the following to your browser window and follow the instructions: https://twitter.com/#!/ProverseBooks

'Like us' on Facebook: www.facebook.com/ProversePress

Request our E-Newsletter
Send your request to info@proversepublishing.com.

Availability
Most titles are available in Hong Kong and world-wide from our Hong Kong based Distributor, The Chinese University Press of Hong Kong, The Chinese University of Hong Kong, Shatin, NT, Hong Kong SAR, China. Email: cup-bus@cuhk.edu.hk

All titles are available from Proverse Hong Kong and the Proverse Hong Kong UK-based Distributor.

We have stock-holding retailers in Hong Kong, Singapore (Select Books), Canada (Elizabeth Campbell Books), Principality of Andorra (Llibreria La Puça, La Llibreria).

Orders can be made from bookshops in the UK and elsewhere.

Ebooks
Most of our titles are available also as Ebooks.

www.ingramcontent.com/pod-product-compliance
Lightning Source LLC
Chambersburg PA
CBHW062114080426
42734CB00012B/2867